This book belongs to:

. . . .

. . . .

How to use this book:

Alphablocks helps children learn to read, from their first encounter with letters and sounds to independent reading. It is all about engaging children's interest and having fun with words. *R's Rough Ride* introduces children to three new letters and sounds, as taught in Reception and in some Nursery classes: **E**, **U** and **R**. This book is designed for an adult and child to enjoy together. Here are some tips:

• Call the Alphablocks by their letter sounds, not by their letter names - this helps your child learn the letter sounds.

• Try to say a short **rrr**!, not 'ruh'. The vowel sound **e** is the starting sound of 'echo' and **u** is the starting sound of 'up'.

• Try running your finger along the words as you read: this gives your child the idea of how reading works. After a few reads, encourage your child to read the letter sounds to you.

• The magic words the Alphablocks make are for your child to read. Tap each Alphablock and say its sound, then blend the sounds to read the whole word.

Reading should be a fun experience and never a chore. Be sure to catch your child in the right mood and let them tell you when they've had enough. You can use the activities at the back of the book as a reward for great reading!

You can find out more about Alphablocks and reading at **www.alphablocks.tv**

First published in Great Britain in 2015 by Egmont UK Limited,
The Yellow Building, 1 Nicholas Road, London W11 4AN

Original illustrations © Alphablocks Ltd 2010-2015
Alphablocks logo © Alphablocks Ltd 2010

ISBN 978 1 4052 7837 9
59913/1
Printed in Italy

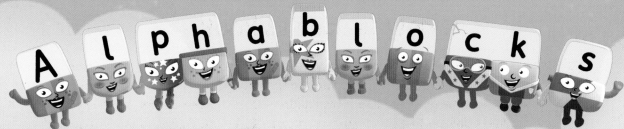

R's Rough Ride

There's a sound in Alphaland – **rrr**! It's the red pirate **R**, riding in on her rope.

"Ready for a pirate adventure?" she roars.

Can you make a **r**! **r**! **r**! sound, like **R**? It's the sound **R** makes when she **roars**.

"**u**! **u**! **u**! Unfair," shrugs **U**.
"We haven't got a pirate ship!"

"**g**! **g**! **g**! I've got a good idea,"
grins **G**.

R, **U** and **G** team up and ...

Can you make an **u**! **u**! **u**! sound, like **U**? It's the sound **U** makes when he means **unfair**!

Help **R**, **U** and **G** do **word magic**.

r-u-g, rug!

"A rug will make a really good ship," roars **R**. "But now we'll need some more Alphablocks to help us."

"**o**! **o**! **o**!" says O, offering to help.

d! **d**! **d**! **D** dashes in. "Let's do it!"

R, **O** and **D** team up and ...

Help **R, O** and **D** do **word magic**.

r-o-d, rod!

A rod, for a pirate ship's mast.

"Nearly ready," says **R**. "But real ships need a sail."

a! **a**! **a**! And **A** arrives.

With **R**, **A** and **G** here that should be possible ...

Help **R**, **A** and **G** do **word magic**.

r-a-g, rag!

A rag for a sail.
And the ship
is ready!

So the friends set off and before long they see an island.

"**i**! **i**! **i**! I have an idea!" says **I**.

D, **I** and **G** hold hands and ...

Help **D**, **I** and **G** do **word magic**.

d-i-g, dig!

Digging for treasure! They dig and they dig until they find a real treasure chest full of real treasure.

"**e**! **e**! **e**! Excellent!" shouts **E** with a loud echo.

Everyone is excited to have found pirate treasure.

R, **E** and **D** team up and ...

Can you make an **e**! **e**! **e**! sound, like **E**? It's the sound **E** makes when he **echoes**.

Help **R**, **E** and **D** do **word magic**.

r-e-d, red!

A really red sunset! If the sun is setting, that means it's time for the Alphablocks to go home. But how will they get home?

"Unlucky me," moans **U**. "How unfortunate to end up on an island."

"Don't panic," says **P**. "Perhaps I can help."

U and **P** team up and ...

Help **U** and **P** do **word magic**.

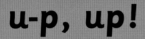

u-p, up!

The Alphablocks all go up and away!
Floating back home. Goodbye roaring
R, unlucky **U** and energetic **E**!

The End

Now turn over to practise everything you've learnt today.

Energetic E!

E is full of energy! Follow the trail so that **E** can exercise and collect all the things that begin with an **e** sound.

Do the action

Cup both hands in front of your mouth and make a big echo, saying **e! e! e!**

Unhappy U

U is under the weather and unhappy. Help cheer **U** up by finishing the umbrella he is under. Finish the umbrella with **u** shapes.

Do the action
Everything is unfair, so shrug your shoulders and moan **u**! **u**! **u**!

Roar with R

R is rather rowdy. Are you ready to be rowdy too? Roar when you see a picture that begins with the **r** sound.

Do the action
Pretend to swing on a rope and get ready to roar **rrr**!

E, U and R are ready!

Match the Alphablocks up with the things that start with their letter sound.

You can read!

Look at all the words you can read now!
Practise reading each of these words.

c - u - p   r - a - t

m - u - d   s - u - m

p - e - t

E, U and **R** say goodbye.
Now you've met them, they'll be
your reading friends for life!

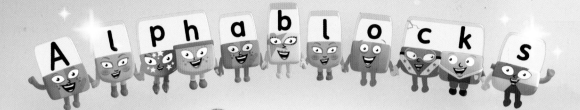

Enjoy all the Alphablocks books!